Mythical Mermaids
Coloring Book

Marty Noble

Dover Publications, Inc.
Mineola, New York

Note

Mermaids and mermen have been featured in stories from cultures all over the world for thousands of years. The very first stories of seafolk can be traced back to Greek and Babylonian mythology, and they have since been passed down and dispersed through folklore, much in the same way that tales of fairies and dragons have. Although the tales differ depending on where they are told, mermaids in modern folklore share some common features—human from the waist up and fish from the waist down, they are invariably depicted as being beautiful, having alluring voices, and are usually linked to the disappearance of ships, sailors, men, or children. Inside this unique coloring book you will find 30 ready-to-color illustrations of merfolk, each one from a different myth or folktale, and accompanied by a brief caption explaining the tale from which he or she comes.

Bibliographical Note

Mythical Mermaids Coloring Book is a new work, first published by
Dover Publications, Inc., in 2012.

International Standard Book Number
ISBN-13: 978-0-486-48169-2
ISBN-10: 0-486-48169-7

Manufactured in the United States by RR Donnelley
48169707   2015
www.doverpublications.com

Atargatis comes from one of the oldest known mermaid stories, recorded in 1000 B.C. Assyria.
Atargatis was a goddess who unintentionally killed a shepherd after falling in love with him.
Ashamed of this terrible deed, she jumped into a lake where she took the form of a mermaid.

In Greek and Philistine stories **Derceto** is the mermaid goddess of fertility. She shares a similar story to *Atargatis,* and is considered representative of the moon.

Irish merfolk, known as **merrows,** shapeshift between human and mermaid forms using a magical cap called a *cohuleen druith.*

The Russian *rusalka* are the spirits of young women who have been murdered. They are said to use song to lure men and children to the sea in order to drown them.

The *sirens* of Greek mythology sing beautiful songs in order to lure sailors to the coast of their rocky island. The boats are inevitably shipwrecked along the shore, and the sirens trap the men there forever.

The Little Mermaid is a Danish fairytale about a young mermaid who is willing to exchange her beautiful voice for a pair of legs after she falls in love with a human prince.

Orkneyjar comes from the Orkney Islands in the United Kingdom. One of the *finfolk,* she was doomed to grow uglier and uglier unless she could attract—or trap—a human man and make him her husband.

The Celtic mermaid originated in a tale called *The Old Man from Cury*, which tells the story of an old man who, while wandering along the shore, saw a mermaid sitting on a rock admiring herself. When she looked up and saw the old man, she slipped back into the ocean.

In this popular legend, Alexander the Great's sister, **Thessalonike** turns into a mermaid after seeming to have drowned. She lived in the Aegean Sea where passing sailors would be required to answer her question, "Is Alexander the King still alive?" in order to pass on safely.

In the Italian legend of ***The Siren Wife***, the beautiful wife of a sailor is left home alone for a long period of time while her husband is away at sea. When her husband returns and finds her with a rich count, he throws her into the sea. There she is found by a group of sirens and transformed into one of them.

The merman from Wales, **Morgan**, abducts wandering children who stray to close to his lake. This tale was likely made up to keep children from going near deep water while unattended.

In this story from the United Kingdom, a young man with a beautiful voice enchanted the *Mermaid of Zennor* with his songs. He then left the land to live with her under the waters.

The Seal Maiden is a Celtic legend in which a young seal is forced to live on land as a human girl after disobeying her mother. After she is grown and married, her young son discovers his mother's history, and becomes her link to the world she left behind.

When the son of a Maori chief in New Zealand marries the beautiful mermaid *Pania*, no one believes him since she must disappear into the sea during the daylight hours. When a village elder tells him that feeding Pania a morsel of human food will keep her on the land forever, he tries to slip some into her mouth while she sleeps. But it is no use, for when the sea creatures see this, they call out a warning and Pania is swept back into the ocean.

A French count named Raymond meets and marries a beautiful girl named *Melusina* despite her strange condition that he stay away from her on Saturdays. Eventually, Raymond begins have jealous suspicions and, on spying on Melusina one Saturday, finds her to have turned into a fish from the waist down. When Melusina learns of his spying she disappears, returning occasionally as a specter to haunt her husband's castle.

The Haitian *Lasirén* is one of three mermaid sisters who represent women's personalities. One sister is cool and calm, the other angry and strong. Lasirén is a blend of the two.

Aycayai was a Carribean girl so beautiful that she robbed all the men of their free will. At first the other women of the community exile her, but the men follow Aycayai. Eventually she is condemned to live in the sea as a mermaid.

In the tale of *The Fish Husband*, a beautiful Nigerian girl falls in love with a merman. The two marry, and the wife calls her husband to her every night by singing a song at the riverbank. When the girl's father finds out she married without his permission, he kills the fish man. The girl is so sad that she jumps into the river, where she is transformed into a mermaid.

River Mumma lives in the waters around Jamaica where she guards the Golden Table. Sometimes the table will rise to the surface during low tide, but the greedy should not be tempted to steal it—anyone who tries is pulled into the waters and drowned by River Mumma.

Yemaja is the Nigerian water goddess who is considered to be the mother of all aquatic life. Without her existence, sea creatures could not survive. Yemaja literally means "mother whose children are like fishes."

Mami Wata is the mermaid goddess of beauty. If spotted by a mortal, she transports them to her underwater realm, where they gain great spiritual understanding and are then returned to earth where they grow wealthier and more attractive.

The **Warsaw Mermaid** lived in the waters off the coast of Poland where she annoyed the fishermen by letting the fish out of their nets. Eventually, she was captured by a man who intended to show her off as an exhibit at the town fair. When the young son of a fisherman heard about this, he felt bad for the mermaid and set her free. In her gratitude she vowed to protect the little fishing village (now the city of Warsaw) forever.

The Scottish *Muir-Bigh* is a supernatural being that will grant three wishes to anyone who captures her. Her fish tail is a covering that can be removed when she wants to take the form of a human and come on to the land. If she loses the fish tail covering (or if it is taken from her) she can no longer return to the sea.

A poor German miller lost everything and was about to throw himself in the lake, when a *nixie* appeared before him, and offered to make him rich in exchange for his first-born son. The miller agreed, and immediately became rich. He told his wife of his promise, but she did not want to give up her baby. The boy grew to manhood, but was eventually swept under the waters by the mermaid while hunting near the shore.

When a young Ukrainian boy falls in love with the beautiful *Nastasia of the Sea* he must complete a series of impossible tasks in order to win her. Luckily, his magical horse gives him some much-needed aid, and he eventually marries the lovely mermaid.

Oannes is the Babylonian sea god who taught man the arts, sciences, and written language. He is said to have come to earth from a place similar to the mythical Atlantis.

The story of the Indonesian water spirit, *Nyai Roro Kidul* begins while she was a human girl so beautiful that the jealous women of the town curse her with black magic and make her hideous. She then has a dream that jumping into the water will cure her of the curse. When she does, the curse breaks, and she is transformed into a mermaid — and becomes even more beautiful than she was before.

The Passamaquoddy Indian legend tells the story of the *Ne Hwas*—girls who were transformed into mermaids after swimming into deep, enchanted water.